The Crooked Floor

Also by T M Collins

Poetry

My Poetry
The Poetic Totem
Yabby Creek
Along the Lip's Edge
House of Voices
The Ruined Room
The Cold Stones of Feeling

Fiction

Until a Shrimp Learns to Whistle

T M Collins

The Crooked Floor

For Zachary and Bridget

The Crooked Floor
ISBN 978 1 76109 437 8
Copyright © text T M Collins 2009
Cover image: Max Vakhtbovych from Pexels

First published 2009 by Ilura Press

This edition published 2022 by
GINNINDERRA PRESS
PO Box 3461 Port Adelaide 5015
www.ginninderrapress.com.au

Contents

The Crooked Floor	9
In Downpours	10
Time's Reticence	11
Moon Spit	12
Reading Your Book	14
Shipping Containers	16
That Night At the Powerhouse	17
The Dirigible Over Suburbia Circa 1985	18
White Hat	20
The Continual Breaking of Fragile Glass	24
The House of Doors	29
Time Bleeds As She Walks Past	32
At Each Turn of Years	34
A Snake In the Grass	36
Images of Australia: a Suite of Poems (Part 2)	37
I Want	45
Part of a Shadow	46
The Circus	47
Alone In a Mirrored Ballroom	48
That Night In Townsville	49
Three Photographs Never Taken	51
Damage	53
Hammered Into Heaven	54
Walking a Crop Circle	56
Moments That Show	58
The Inspiration of Trees	60
Warmth	67
Days and Counting	69
After That First Time	71
Boot Scraper Mess	72

My Brother Visits Home	74
People I See Walking	80
Knocks At the Door and Poetry	82
Acknowledgements	83

Even then I knew it was a taunt,
a match held up to the birdcage,
where the hawk sat on a stick.
                      Frank Huyler, 'The Blood of Strangers'

The Crooked Floor

'Not drunk is he who from the floor
Can rise alone, and still drink more;
But drunk is he who prostrate lies,
Without the power to drink or rise.'
– T.L. Peacock, *Misfortunes of Elphin*

The floor's crooked he'd say,
the sweat of blood in his eyes,
his senses in a slow trampolining,

his face white and smudged red,
the raised roll lines of the veins
at his temple, the trembling hands,

his breath like pit gas, the eyebrows
hunching, holding up a rack of frowns.
'Dad' I'd yell but nothing just

the cold insistence of my voice,
then the chill creak of the side
gate every so often, the wind

riding it back and forth, then
no wind, no sound, nothing
expected, like an empty bottle.

In Downpours

'Small things can pit
the memory like a cyst.'
– James McAuley

Today's downpour reminded
me how the old yard could
turn into a paddock of childhood.

Summer attuning its light like
leaves, we as kids running, staying
play-active, avoiding evening, when

the setting in the west would promote
calls of 'Come inside now please.'
We'd come in, our faces brimming red,

our gestures all slack from laughter.
I'd always look up at the roundness
of the clock, its two black teeth oddly

hanging in the sniggering mouth – 5.35 p.m.
And behind me in the cooling yard
I believed men were pulling darkness

over the neighbourhood, lonely men
ready for other things, they'd be
clicking padlocks on gates and

thumping furnace doors shut as
I had a bath and felt the blind of
tiredness creep down over me.

Time's Reticence

'The waters wear the stones.'
– Old Testament

I rather not believe the years had
cranched over and over to a fine
powder of cement at the wall base.

The tap nestled amongst a furnace
of ferns, heat and rising moisture
from the ground like invisible mist.

The tap, nine rows of bricks up from
the slivered grass ends had dripped
for as long as I could remember.

Mitchell was seven (he's now 45) and
we'd fill straws with drips of water then
spit blow the contents at lizards on the

side fence, never needing to turn the tap;
it'd been wrenched fist tight, brass against
rubber against metal thread, someone trying

to close the gap, stop that infuriating drip.
Now all those years later the tap still drips.
He never much once watered the lawn.

Just walked to the bus, leather railway bag
scuffing his brown trouser leg, and now
he's old but still younger than that tap.

Moon Spit

for Grandma Linen

As a boy I'd often sit watching:

Six o'clock, the tea cooling, the neat faded curtains
fan touch-tipping the cup handle on the side table,
a table stained and polished over years of years,
the white cat blacked-eyed asleep on her lap,
purring like soup simmering, grandma's breath
curdling from last nights sherried saliva, but her
mind does less now; the curtain edges do more
with their wave buffet, then suddenly dead still, then
wave buffet again, little air eddies occasionally making
her eyes blink slit open closed, nervous tremor
while outside, the sky is a mark of respect, still and grey.

Fish in the tank on the long table wiggle and gulp-mouth
water, their eyes dead gazes, their scaled torsos trembling
lines of lance-light as stained moonlight begins cluttering
the floor like moth's spore on a black jacket, evening is
ink dirty from smog of the city's workday drudge.

She jumps and starts as she sleeps, her muscles in a
slow stamp following wantonly behind 'old man
time', he's caught up with her and begins to lap, and
the soup is shrinking in the pot, the cat's fur now a
settled soft down and I'm no longer a little boy.

As clocks elbow six thirty her trembling breath
has a sound to it, a resonance dead of desire, her once
sudden lust of life now the creeping vine clung to fading
green downpipes, images, flashes to be remembered,
transformed into forged thoughts, fevered memories
of an old lady who was once mother, once a daughter
and her lust for life was so evident in the comment
said so often as I grew up, on clear nights with the
moon pregnant in the night's belly she'd say
'Look at that moon spit on the table,
is it not such a beautiful sight young man.'

Reading Your Book

for Bronwyn

I don't call myself a poet, because I
don't like the word. I'm a trapeze artist.'
– Bob Dylan

A skitter skatter of blood like some exploded
little insect's body on the book's page's edge.

I was reading your poetry to the illustrator
before we'd made love, a love where no map

exists and suddenly my finger hit the plain slit
end of the room blind, at first a stutter of blood

then a bleeding seep, I remembered my father
cutting his eye with the slither edge of a sheet

of paper late at night, mother once a nurse,
again met her most horrid fear, a bleeding eye

where each movement pushes out a neat blob
of blood, the excruciating pain of the purple

pigeon blood pulse of colour in night's darkness.
Blood in its journey to air changes colour much

like the leaves in the Black Forests of Europe,
as if they have an inkling, a personality. But now

here I am a tissue wrapped about my crying finger,
and I'm thinking of you, your words, you, after

having made love to her and having read your
poetry to her. Isn't it funny how poetry can

become that trapeze cable, that tightrope wire,
taut tight, tethered end to end, or coloured

abseiling ropes plumb bobbing legged torsos below.
Isn't it amazing that here I am the morning after,

realising that your words were the bridge in the
moment last night, an intoxicating communion.

Shipping Containers

If I could put all my life's detritus
in a cold shipping container, all the
sad wick and spark of life's existence,

the sorrowful vestments one wears, and
the coming stain of old age, everything I

didn't want, put it all in a cold shipping
container then lug it on a truck the few
miles or so to the sea, the contents bleating

and bulging the sides and, in the rear-vision
mirror there it'd be heavy and solid, its

metal riveted seams staring back at me
as I tipped the lever expelling it into the
sea, if only I had a shipping container.

That Night At the Powerhouse

'And now this pale swan in her watery nest
Begins the sad dirge of her certain ending.'
– Shakespeare

Your sandstone hair coloured the black
grace of evening, the resting river, baying
slowly, strobingly at the shoreline, it was a
time to be written about (you away from him).

It could have been your wedding night,
you were that beautiful and the spelling
of your sensuality was in the way you
leaned against the wall as we kissed, your

tongue slim, soft and wet with warm intent,
your thighs all tensioned up as we pulsed
together, but the trip home in the cab had
the thistles of guilt growing in your every

breath, we sat apart in the cold back seat
of that cab, the cabbie wanted us to embrace
and harpsichord his lonely cold night drive
in the rear-view mirror…

and then not needing

a dictionary, I realised the way you got out
of the cab was the sheer epitome of rejection.
You walked to your home, to him, walked
slowly like the last refrain in a funeral dirge.

The Dirigible Over Suburbia Circa 1985

Sam didn't see Dad hit veranda decking, he was bucketing mulberries, the purple stain ringing his mouth and nicotining his fingers the colour of pigeon blood. This time of year, in deepest valleys of winter the brewery blimp would lump across our weld of sky, a moving fixture, its body no Norman Lindsay fulsome nude but a huge distended olive floating in a blue sea, the thing making stamp-lick speed, and on a day without clouds, was it coming, going or just becalmed.

No one noticed his bulging temple, throbbing like a snake breathing its entire body, no one noticed the vein relax then seconds later bulge out once more, each time it relaxed on the outside, on the inside it was a ballooning blimp in his head, eventually bursting inwards, an exploding fireball of energy, a Hindenburg pulse. That tumour, a powerful tap root tendrilling, choking the main pumping veins, arteries, gathering them together fist-like, a soldier holding a bunch of detonator fuse sticks.

He fell swiftly, body slack and loose, lost of form, sunken in at neck, eyes and chest as if an explosion obliterated parts of the inside frame of his body, vaporised them so he lost the firmness that gave him shape, like ripping a huge tree from ground, the soil sucked into the gaping hole, and his eyes were open, a fish's cold stare. Like an anchor hitting water, Mum with penicillin eyes stood dishevelled in housekeeping clothes, her apron a hive of germs, pockmarked stains like potholes in a disused airfield.

I sat that night in the exact spot, looking out at neighbourhood darkness, my thoughts half hung on shrubs, the clothesline, the fence, resting my toes (like he did) on the protruding, jutting edge of a too-long floorboard. 'Never trimmed off,' he'd said. 'I'll trim it up to the others one day.' The night sky was a torn stage curtain, moth eaten spots where jagging splinters of light escaped, sinking backstage to scatter and soak into the weathered wood boards. He was gone, a dead language like Latin.

Looking up I could smell wetness, soon the blinking stage lights of night sky were fused out by heavy silver chain-mail curtains of rain falling from the rafters, those same rafters that tethered the blimp earlier today. The rain fell, dissolving into the peatmoss coloured yard, rills of water on the paving, everything distorted in a blur of weak-lit rain, a black velvet sky, my tongue between my teeth pushing back tears, and the Exit sign in the shopping centre driveway next door bleeding

rain down its plastic casing had me wiping tears and rain-wash from my face, my hands fisted in my pockets, shoulders turned in like fenders on an old Valiant, making me ask the cold wet question, 'Are all exits as cold, sudden and sinister as this?' It was ten years later, the house up for sale, the last day of occupancy, old Mick the carpenter trimming up that floorboard. Handing the small block of wood to Mum, she clamped it tight, closed her fingers over the memories, the years, over everything.

White Hat

for the artist Betty Eastman

As I'm washing up and noticing
a lemonade sky filtered with streaks
of blue light I realise that I'm not
foretold to trivial dustings of daily
life and understand you're not meant
to mention in poems, are you, one's
day to day troublesome trawlings
like they are some local sport report.

But today after the computer failed
and having last night helped a woman
with a spotted eye patch change a flat tyre
on the road outside my unit, the night
hanging from her like frost left by ghosts,
I went mid-morning to the Red Hill art gallery,
wandering and gazing, looking for something,
looking for a feeling, for something emotional to buy.

Most annoyingly, more a pestering,
I found a painting titled *White Hat*
or should I say, I found you, you seemed
to have some magnetic life, and I was
unsure of its intention, good or bad.
In the car on the way home, you were not happy,
and I was certainly aware you hated being covered
in the tight dry skin of brown paper with that
icky bubble wrap beneath, on release I sat you
gently with awe on the black leather chair.

You were not happy there,
I couldn't find a place where your lonely look
didn't judge and follow me throughout the house,
knew you needed to be hung on the grey walls,
in a prominent place on these grey walls,
walls that have been touched by the muses of my five obsessions,
Poetry, Art, thoughts of *Elizabeth*, the *music patterns*
that for years have bounced and tufted themselves into the
gyprock texture and the *solemn voices* of my parents at their
lonely last visit, bringing me warmed food in a dish covered
with alfoil.

Whispering (in a corner out of view),

*I honestly feel this painting has been tinkered to incredibly nasty
and sinister Lolita like thoughts and the painting mount is such
an unusual colour, nothing I've seen before, it I think changes
shade every now and again, like it has some bit of struggling
infant life. It is a stunning deep pastel blue then a green and it
often matches the colour of the patches of worry under the young
girl's eyes.*

Betty, I ask you now, why paint this girl
in such mock peasant attire with looks
of disgust, distrust and fear falling down
her face and on glancing back these
feelings and images are still hung at her eyes,

hung like a sticky length of plastic boot lace tape
on an iron railing at the edge of a
football field, where the open spaces
are oddly vacant and lonely.

Each time I look, they hang, menacing
in their metaphor of something else,
some hidden reason, leaving some
mystery, doubt, like for instance, why
with such night flight credentials
does the flying fox drench itself over
blackened power lines like discarded death.

Betty do you expect me to simply
believe that this is just portrait of a
young girl wearing a white hat.

'Try to find, you fool,' it says to me,
some place of prominence.
I''m supposed to find
a place where it can bother
whoever passes it, pestering
everyone ever endlessly so that
one night after having had enough
I will just lock it away in
a dark time shadowed cupboard
behind the old leather jacket,
hangered football jerseys and
my aunt's old frocks and hats.

What happened in her life, Betty,
what was it that you've incarcerated,
captured from her life and so deeply,
so deeply sullied in oil on canvas.

What is it?

The Continual Breaking of Fragile Glass

Drifting

If from the water's throat we looked
above the rut and rip of bay current
through the language of water and patience
watched the boy fishing, his hands numb wet
and above the sky black and spittle-specked.

Watched him shuffle, push soles of feet
into shoes like suction cup weights,
canvas shoes braced against the jetty's planked lip,
and with the faint smell of salt and seaweed the moon
spilled its light, dancing a residue on the black surface.

On that jetty he's much like a little trinket person
in a dome of glass with a backdrop of weak lit light.

His thoughts are heavy terracotta
scholaring the roof of recent despair,
the line uselessly limp, its deadness
drawn away resembling a loose stitch
pulled through an expanse of black silk,
and the wind does snigger in cold response.

The boy thinks and talks to himself
the line in his fingers coir like
now heavy with dried salt and
air's locked sea slime particles.

Thinks of his mother waking suddenly
in the early ditch of night with a wet pillow,
his father's knob of terror about to enter.

Children decipher late at night, not from seeing
but by capturing words and slogging them
over time from out of fuzzy nightmare pictures.

Now these thoughts are charged away by
the ear-chilling sou'westerly tugging the line
back to plumb bob depths below his feet.

Someone away in the distant air is chummering
an outboard motor in roar service,
then the chunter chunter sound
as the boat smacks through water
the stars clicking dark on and off.
The boy listens as the pylons are
slimy white in the hungry moonlight.

He is alone with thoughts at the
back of his eyes, all else is landscape
distilling night-time talk.

Caught

The wind was rumouring and murmuring agonies of the day's heat, and now such a nameless night, lost without the linen stained moon, it had

gone, a slipped disc into the pocket of this the blackest night. The boy had caught his fish and on the jetty planking beneath his sneakered

shoe one solid black lustrous eye looked up at the stars, blinking a secret code of patent death. The boy was blindfolded in his intentions,

his little palms and fingers unable to hold the fishes struggling might so with the rusted blunted knife he stabbed and pierced the silvered

head. Now as he ran the dull blade back and forth scything skips of scales jumping and jackknifing at his feet, the night's voice off in the

distant distant dark was familiar, like the continual breaking of fragile glass. And in the yellow velvet mouth was the brassed hook,

clean through the stretched fabric of the lip, he wiggled and gently jolted, and with a little pluck it was out, then with that knife he slowly

letter opened the length of pursed belly, scrape-flicking the contents, all the time wondering why his father let the handbrake off.

The Car

It still looked like a car, nose deep in the swollen rocks,
the tide well out, crabbing the outer sand bars until dusk.

As they winched it up, the red splatter on the inside
windscreen was visible like a birthmark.

His arms like pegs draped over the steering wheel.

Birdshit and Rust

At the end of a chill evening's fishing
he walked the creel up the charcoal-
coloured jetty; one arm each carrying
the wickered basket of cold dead weight,
heavy droplets of bay water tapping
every so often at his sneakered feet.

The Park light dead in its cracked casing,
he'd clean them at home in the laundry.
His mother sat sequestered at the kitchen table,
the table pulled across to patch itself against the
filthy sink, she'd spit, and again and each time
the teacup of straw-coloured grog would shake
and her cold dry crying socket screwed eyes
stared a reminder of years of pain, stared
like fishes eyes, never asleep, a stare, so cold
and stiff like wrought-iron grotto gate.

He walked to the lean-to laundry,
a patina of frog-coloured mildew on the fibro walls,
the outer wall non-existent, fully open to
the outside landscape – the blue dark road and
thick tree clusters of the Victoria Point Park.

Mosquitoes masqueraded as little sounds making
the big black sounds of night seem darkly
solid and coldly not right, out of place.
Then slowly he eye-pointed at the backyard.

There marooned in knee tickling grass,
the faded blue sedan, the colour of old denim,
its paintwork covered in birdshit and rust,
the tow rope still attached, the windscreen
stain now a faded orange yellow and that
sticker on the back window.

No One Fishes Noah Any More

The House of Doors

It started out as buzzy
fascination with a new front door
(plus some hidden secret reason)
for her place up on Riverington Road,
up that old dirt track, the house
perched bird-like on Bluff West Hill.

But it soon became a compassioned
fit of desire; skin printing ink on her
fingers each weekday, and for hours on
the weekends, stroking and scratching
through the newspapers under
'Demolition' and 'Houses for Removal'.

Within months and always with her dark
hair up in bun, meeting the men who
delivered the doors, telling them to stand
the latest one up against the others whilst
they'd look at her with a quizzical gaze.

Occasionally one would ask
'How many doors you got there lady?'
She'd never answer.
But word had it, around 400.

School kids at the local primary
school said there was thousands,
doors from all over the world.

Then on the 18th June other men
arrived very early, and began
assembling planked scaffolding
around the outer shell
of the weatherboard house,
by Wednesday it was a
house fortressed by a
network of metal piping.

People said she didn't work,
said she'd got an inheritance, and
that way back, something bad
had happened, and that she only ever
ventured out on rare occasions
like some obscure snail peeking
out from its shell.
The men stripped and pried
the outer weatherboards from
the inner frame of the house
leaving a swollen red roof
hanging glumly as each day
people wandered up from the
village, traipsing up to gawk
and stretch their heads like turtles
eyeing a beach.

By the Saturday 332 doors
had been placed, positioned
side to side; end to end, like
tiles all around the framework,
doors of all colours and designs,
some with small glass panels at the top,
many with knobs and handles still on,
stained doors, bare wood, some coloured
brightly in gloss, others dulled in matt.

On Sunday with the sun monkeying
up the trunk of the sky, all was quiet.
It was odd, strange, very different,
you didn't have to look for long
for the image memory to stay forever
in your mind, where else would you see
something as peculiar as this.

Finally it must be said,
we all knew her name but
it didn't seem right to name her
in a poem, it was enough to say
the rumour was that she'd lost
her young son many years
earlier and it had something
to do with doors, doors.

'There was a door to which I found no key:
There was a veil past which I could not see.'
– Edward Fitzgerald

Time Bleeds As She Walks Past

Inside the night sky is a torn stage curtain,
moth eaten spots, where jagging splinters
of light escape, sinking backstage to scatter
and soak into the weathered wood boards,
I sit outside at the entrance carousel suddenly

realising like an anchor hitting water that our
love is a dead language like Latin. I miss you,
and right now the thought that is retelling over

and over like a burning wick is the susurration
of your breathing as I love you with the warm
tip of my tongue and later, on those nights, you
would rest your temple on my tummy and do the
same to me, why this particular snatched bit of our

time together and not some other, it is like a
roulette wheel, many things come up. Looking up
and drawing wet night air in I notice that the blinking

stage lights of the night sky are gone, fused out by
the heavy silver chain-mail curtain of rain falling from
the rafters and dissolving into the peatmoss coloured
pavement as you walk towards me, your pace not
slowed by the rill of water on the ground, you pass me,

in a blur of weak lit rain, with black velvet top and the
pigeon blood skirt hugging your angles, my tongue between
my teeth pushing back tears, but it is the Exit sign

bleeding rain down its plastic casing that has me
wiping tears and rain-wash from my face, my hands
fisted in my pockets, shoulders turned in like fenders
on an old Cadillac and making me ask the cold wet
night air, if all exits are as cold, sharp and sinister as this.

At Each Turn of Years

for Karen Johnson

They say the moon can trouble our blood,
on full moon nights, creeping cats in our veins,
thoughts and desires like spinning stars.
An old lover once told me at times of stress
let your thoughts dance with the moon.
I remember sitting on the driveway at
Dorinda and Douglas Streets looking up
through the tunnelled aperture of the
telescope Dad bought, seeing those craters,
my thoughts and desires for hours after like
delicate feet lifting, dancing, dolceing through moist
tipped grass, ideas wandering and wimping about
in my head, thinking of Orville and da Vinci and
church, new football boots, school and Tiger the
Basset Hound. Now, my thoughts in concert with
the moon, but my thoughts are more like the
troubled blood in a wild animal's body, thoughts
of my broken love, my children's future, and, that
lack of fruitful freedom of thought, more a
troubled list of needs, wants and desires, hopes
for the future. To be nine years old again with
the kindred glow of moon flushing down the
insides of that telescope to court my inspiration,
dance my mind's visions, polished, free and
innocent. The moon has taught me one thing, that
through life we learn new dances at each turn of years,

each chunk-down weight of the cog-worn birthday
movement, the raised metal wear line in our heads as we
know we are growing old; and, over each turn of years
whether it be the creeping cats in a child's veins
or the troubled blood of those wild animals,
all is simply moonlight glow to show life's journey.
Gathering age like dust collected on light bulbs
in the basement of an old factory, that saw men's,
women's hands, foreheads wrinkle with age,
I remember what that lover said, allow the glow
to enter your heart like those delicate feet lifting
through moonlit grass from youth to old age.
Tonight outside, at the end of this day,
what shapeless shadows tree my peaceful
thoughts amid September, the most beautiful
month where winter's cold tongue and dry
mouth has quietened allowing moonlight
through the window blanketing my desk
in a warm cloudy glow, covering my thoughts, covering.

A Snake In the Grass

With real earthenware feelings upwards over time
from the bottommost part of my desire
I gave all through love's hidden trials

but you,
shod in a cold pensive selfishness
returned a lazy love.

Like a cat still with nine lives
not much mattered but the latest
Vanity Fair and the urchin shows on TV,

and while all this was,
as you liked to call it
'the best of suburban romance',

your son sat upstairs in his room alone,
calculating his mother's true love and
perhaps wondering at age twelve

why men and women play out
such silly creative games of commitment,
the touching, the fondling, the kissing, while becoming
in the process good liars and cheats,
he could see each day the cold and useless reality
of disposable 'white goods' relationships.

Images of Australia: a Suite of Poems (Part 2)

1. Laneway

the old man with dry ice eyes
colour drained in a long youth
now a threadbare talent propped
amongst laneway boxes, awake.

2. Girl in a Skivvy

she casts her elbow out, the
flute glass holds petrol-coloured
wine, her blue skirt is tinged with
cat hair, a hurried night out, but
it's the smile on her face like a
split olive that has her alone.

3. Midday at Yeronga

a crow flies in front of a Telstra tower,
a black armband of purpose as the
sun's naked glow and the after tow of
thought has pigeons pavement pecking.

4. Waiting

there is truck idling, smoke fumes drifting back
under the chassis, hiding, not wanting to be known
as pollution as a young girl stands demurely at the
bus seat, the truck levels off leaving her covered
in heavy white smoke like a bad dream.

5. Collapse

like an anchor hitting water she
fell in the middle of us, suddenly
cold and the susurration of her
breathing faint, and the memory
is – the lift lights slipping through
each floor like a slow burning wick.

6. Strength

for Vera Newsom

wildflowers sated by
wind and freedom
clasped in day's cool
glow and night's heavy
army blanket.

7. A Census of Smells

a dog named Alien paw pedals
the garden verge sniffing sniff
sniffing, dictionarying the yard,
a lexicon of different smells, his
vocabulary immense especially
after the stickiness of summer rain.

8. In a Field

a boy does not look up. A tinge of
pink in the sky records coldness. He
sits amongst waist high grass tips, pods,

clusters of tiny sods, seeds, mistaking
themselves as souls of the grass stalks,
they call them pollen, those faint orange
green clusters. The boy does not look up.

9. Departures

a woman leaves through the exit gate at Canberra
airport and the syllables of her hair sing in the
breeze, cavorting about her face as a date block
calendar flips a few pages in the sultry air,
another outnumbered calendar day departure.

10. Boarding School

there was the snib on the door and
downstairs the slow turning of clocks,
tuning themselves against each cranking
cog to arm, while night crept beneath
blurred stars, rain began perspexing the sky,
a man held a young boys shoulder blades.

11. Coolangatta, Queensland

clouds kapok the sky, rain stretched
tight across the skyline night, neon lights
drowning in their dissolving colour as the
ambulance all fast of sound tunnels sirens
into our night, echoing on, echoing on.

12. Laidley 4.15 a.m.

the foreman telling pickers
to leave the twig on the apple,
it remains fresher like a clean mirror.

13. Billinudgel, NSW

the moon is not tonight stained linen
but drum-skin tight and off colour
like an old white naval uniform.

14. Sea Eagle

jumps down Batman like, wings
counter sprung to one third
extension, cape partially extended,
a moderate dump down onto the thin
shock absorber legs, then a hurried
walk across the darkened expanse.

15. Rundle Street, Adelaide

heavy clouds detour south as tears
sign themselves on a young girl's face,
a slight tinge of sting as she hugs her
brother goodbye, she's leaving home.

16. Tweed River

houses sit like oyster shells amidst the
hillsides, seagulls heel push
into honeyed sand, the sky freshly painted

asa plane stencils 'free drinks' at the
'Playroom' before 6 p.m., when
all the crabs are out and about.

17. Pottsville Beach

the moon sits as an arc of frost,
invisible sacks of heat move in as
the surf saws and pumps inward.

18. West End, 1974

a young boy with sun burnt face pulls
a home-made trailer behind his
bike and on that trailer is a
water-tinted wooden clock.

19. The Grandfather Clock

it just floats, its chime dissolved,
diluted and finally drowned in the
flux of flood water, to rest heavy
and muddy on the slippery bank.

20. Wedding

the sky is like a fresco, backdrop
of pastel brilliance yet on the roadside
verge resting ornamental, a bouquet from
two weeks back, the flowers all feathered
and wilting in brown decay, meaningless.

21. Hospital Bed

a held hand and in a dying ear is said
a lonely thank you and goodbye as
the Mr Whippy van plays its ugly tune
outside on a road festooned with cars.

22. Creek Bank

a mud wasp patrols the bank, stitching
back and forwards lines of interest, its
wings racing time to find a spot in
the mud walls where it can bury life.

23. Sunset

the orange and raspberry of the sun's
juices staining the sky and everywhere
things are slowing, even the sun
burnt glow on the river is fading.

24. Old House

across the splintered floorboards
and cobwebs that watch from above,
every movement stirs dust from its face
down sleep and the smell is of the past.

25. From the Plane Window

building roofs like stuck on scatters of tin foil,
streets and roads, map lines drawn by blind
cartographers, colours trick themselves in

the sunlight into shadows, perforations of
shade dot the landscape flat shades of green,
grey and brown as vehicles welter along
black tracks resembling exposed open pulses.

26. Mountains After Rain

today they are bluey green with more blue
than green but they look clean, yesterday
they were the dusty hides of elephants.

27. A Man

fingers and rubs lottery ticket between his
thumb and index finger, dreaming of winter
holiday thoughts as the traffic throbs a low breath.

28. Foreboding

clouds full of lightning fear and dread, their
dank dance of posturings across the afternoon
sky, the sun a sick oyster in the storm water's
murky deep as in the distance thunder walks and
lightning cracks and hits, flecking the sky with words.

29. The Band

the music of colour and sound
like ceramic flowers spinning
in a sculpture garden and amidst
the pouring rain a kookaburra laughing.

30. Wynnum Foreshore Night

the moon a soft cream bubble
amidst the deep black coffee
of this a slow Autumn night.

31. Rocklea Markets, Sunday

a makeshift trestle
the boy's dad selling
coloured toy accordions
the music in his wallet.

To be continued…

I Want

A locket of your hair to
stroke through my fingers.

To sketch the lust line of
your lips with my tongue.

To watch your beauty as you
sleep, to hear your breath,

touch the fullness of your
tummy when those certain

times arrive. To seek
your hugs and kisses, to

turn back time forever
to the time we met, to

live forever in your love,
and I want him to know

everything we did, every
little wanting thing we did.

Part of a Shadow

for Narelle Elizabeth

I knew something was wrong –
her voice on the phone
quavering in loss and despair,
I thought it was her husband,
for a moment I hoped,
but it was her mother.

Her father now wandering around
the house in Toowoomba
having lost half his life shadow
and the body still resting
warm and unmoving on the bed.

I have all this yet before me
so I found it difficult to hold her
tension's hand in supporting grief
in death's cold stave-like stance.

We ended the call with me having
angled the car into the gutter,
the engine purring, the cool
morning air outside whispering
and me wishing that I were her husband,
to hold and kiss her differently,
to catch grief and then percolate it
through a strong loving intent,
to show an unknown side of love,
a love that is kernelled away and
only shown maybe half a dozen times
in a lifetime, in a marriage, a love that is
the equal part of that life shadow.

The Circus

'Nobody should try to play comedy unless they have a circus going on inside.' – David Niven, *The Moon's a Balloon*

She plays the tin whistle, he sits watching,
his posture hegemonic in the extreme, arms
folded, legs crossed, eyes gimlet blue; and above
the heatwaves, the canvas matches this colour.

Accordion at his feet, overgrown toenails
like ivory eyelids; and also at his feet, a child
arranges and rearranges plastic fruit, a pear,
an apple, an orange, pushes them down in

the dirt, and a grape with its stem tight between
index finger and thumb, holds it like holding the
stiffened tail of a dead rat, pushes it too into the
grey dirt, plastic re-vegetating under tent dome

sweat, a hothouse of colour, movement and sound.
Then it is that raw sound of the musical saw and
Coffee-cream like a pan flute, the notes trickling in a
soft silken line from the instrument. With flute,

saw, guitar and eventually, he takes up accordion
side-saddle with Eugene on the snare drum, all these
sounds scold the cold night outside air, scolding
with disfavour, the night is too quiet; pedantry in

black robes as Little Bill in the corner counts the
takings, twice. Right now they are real people,
tomorrow they become the freaks, the lion tamers,
the clowns, jugglers and Bill the ringmaster.

Alone In a Mirrored Ballroom

for Narelle Elizabeth

There is pan flute playing and there are no illusions, no wall mirror
where I can ask for guidance like satellite navigation. I have no idea

why you behave as you do, one minute leavening me in a state of
complete loving intimacy then but two days later after a four-hour drive

you are dripping with guilty despair, that he might know,
find out that I have been as sensual to you, with you as

dusty doves do necking and nudging, nestling their heads
into each other – I do this with my young daughter, rub heads,

hunch our shoulders in the tickling goose-bumpy way, with
my son we used to rub noses, a father showing silly closeness

like those birds on a branch but with you it is more an urge that
overwhelms me, rages me to want to smell you, kiss you,

touch you, to be close to you, on you, within you,
to dance with you, to simply hear your voice and like

those doves to be simply together but alas you are
with him and I have little recourse, another bird in

another tree and as Helmut Berger said 'Sometimes
it is better to just watch what could be.'

That Night In Townsville

The night opens with a wag of breeze
and thoughts of you, the gentle tinkling
tease cuts of your breath at my neck,
my face and then a drink and the night
is taking a topsy-turvy turn with heavy

clouds crawling a detour south. Tears,
signing themselves on my cheeks as an
aberration, run my skin a slight tinge

of sting and as I write this line those
tears flow – 'How often can one person
say I Love You' without some collateral
remnant being heard as tortured birdsong
sung by the forlorn nightbird who travels

as a black shudder in all poet's dreams.
Tap your chest tonight with the shiver I feel
as you rest atop me, the growing shadow

of love seed seeping along the velvet line
of your inner thighs and as the wink and
clink of starlight like glasses together in
that romantic restaurant on the arm of
land at the edge of the sleeping Pacific.

That night the moon was not stained linen
but was the skin on the drumbeat of my heart,
now how often through the twist and curl of

painful thinking, the cold calculus of memory
do I wish I'd pushed you from the cliff,
pushed you that warm night, me hand
coupled in tow to the dark rocks below.
At least then we would have been together.

Three Photographs Never Taken

'A photograph is not only an image (as a painting is an image), an interpretation of the real; it is also a trace, something directly stencilled off the real, like a footprint or a death mask.' – Susan Sontag

1. Terranora Lake Road

His face was daylight robbery
the sheer stuck-in-shock expression,
eyes balled wide, whites watered,
mouth a pried open exclamation,
the nostrils fared and the facial skin
a cold pallid white like paper.

The body crumpled around the
red motor bike and mostly my
mind remembers the grey gravel
stuck in his bloodied hair.

Ambulance and police tended his
mortal needs like worker ants.
Driving off clutching the second
k from *Kawasaki*, my fist gently
nested on the steering wheel.

2. The Chair

The old number was 3229 6304
(now a not-in-service number).

He had an old dentist's chair in the
salon, black leather and heavy chrome.

Late at night opening the back door
with an acquaintance from the pub
entertaining desires wanton needs
in the warm dark soft of that chair.

Years later on meeting my new
lover and hearing her mention the
hair salon in Queen Street with
its big black sinister chair.

3. Pull and Jump

The woman on the edge of the
Tweed River, fishing rod
angled stiffly into the late
day air, the line veed into
muckish brown water.

The line slowly winding in
coated in dried salt slime,
the Alvey reel faintly squeaking,
the rod gently tip buckling,
then hanging below the fat grey sinker
a kid's toy, a palm-sized pink plastic
frying pan, the line tied to its handle.

She didn't like catching fish, thought
it cruel, but she particularly liked the
pulling and jumping feel of the toy
through the water, said it relaxed her.

Damage

for John Andrew Tate

'The Needle and the Damage Done.'
– Neil Young

Often I hear the
click of guns but
later I realise it's
the tapping of the
spoon on the dish,
the vein bulging,
the fist clenched,
eyelids half shut,
trees outside shake
their leaves, cars
srrut dirty paintwork
as the nick happens
and the shitter enters
along a slow blue link
to the brain.

Hammered Into Heaven

She told how he'd come in, always first unbuckle his belt, then place shoes one behind each other in a line, as if they were walking off across a stretch of sand, a roll of notes tied with a dirty string, five, six, seven, seven curled up notes on the dresser.

She told how he'd undress her from behind, kiss her neck, its nasty sandpaper feel, then remove his own clothes, then ease her slowly down on the bed, bent over at the waist.

She told how it would begin slowly, a Morse code like rhythm to it, she'd count over and over the scrolls of woodwork on the bedhead, all the time the half pain at her wrists as she dug a hold into the bedspread and a bit grab of mattress.

She told how he'd move about like a windsurfer, side to side, back, forward, up and down, in and out, rocking at the hips, then the mood would change, he'd auger into her like digging a post hole, deeper and harder, the cold blade in wet soil.

She told how he'd whisper in her ear, 'I'm gonna hamma ya inta heaven,' then he'd hoot and shake like a train, then wasted he'd sit at the wall panting, wide-eyed and sweaty, saying nothing.

She told how she'd remain in position, he'd watch her half bent body shrinking back to size, to normality, to humility, while he was at the wall staring at the centre of her backside, red hand imprints at each buttock.

She told how it was worse at Christmas, she'd have to unwrap the present he'd bought, she'd learned to do it slowly, carefully, not tearing the paper, his breathing all the time like a letter opener prying open a parcel.

She told how her tongue was mashed at the edges, fleshy mounds of scar tissue, she had a habit of chewing her tongue, 'like the cricketers' she said, it helps get through the hours.

She told how each year on her birthday she got a tattoo of a burnt match blue needled into the flesh of her right shoulder blade, a tiny wift of smoke above each blackened head like a surrender banner.

Then she drew down her top to reveal twenty-nine matchsticks dead stencilled on her back.

She told how she still had a few years' matches in her yet.

Walking a Crop Circle

'A map is the dead body of where you've been.
A map is the unborn baby of where you're going.
There are no maps. Maps are pictures of what isn't.'
– Russell Hoban

Knowing how you love maps, I thought you'd be interested
to hear there was no local map in which to locate, find this
place, I found it by mistake, while out driving the English
Midlands, saw it through the passenger window – the sky was
full of ballast,

a smattering of heavy pewter cloud and distantly off were
fragile rainbow strands left floating helplessly from old rain
and the fields all fallen silent, and, there was a heavy wavering
heat like angry tethered horses, then the wind returned,
jocular and frisky, and

the glacial grass was still assailed over, motionless in its bent
diminishment of image even its skeletal flicking shadows had
been wantonly stamped to ground, a springy nest of straw.
Sunlight slipped and shimmered on the surface of my glasses,

then turned back on itself, gone for a second then back
glinting once again, angling in from the side, sharp and bitter
in my eyes. This place was too silent, silence choking on its
own quiet shock and dismay and just my presence and the
simple rhythm of my

breathing – ooo-aaa, ooo-aaa, ooo-aaa. A bird churned past
overhead squawking, its wings making a tent flapping sound.
Now the clouds seemed full of the delicate bones of light
rain, and there was the implausible reek of salt and sea, so far
from the ocean.

Should have taken a photo to show you, to prove it was here
but instead I stood like a cartoon strip character, my face in
mock alarm, eyes with glued disbelief, I imagined you sitting
on the veranda accompanied by only the afternoon's listening
shadows,

the clammy look of your hard-boiled eyes, your old upper lip
furred with sweat, and me telling you how alone I felt in this
giant overseas paddock of bent-over brown yellowing grass,
and how alone you now must feel as you die. Very slowly I
walk the crop circle.

Moments That Show

1.

The man at the cigarette counter
filters his day with anguish,
his wife in new clothes and
late home from work and
of recent early each day to rise.

2.

A woman twirls her wedding ring
with index finger and thumb,
thumbing and fingering it
back and forth like her
need for a decision,
her stare cold and
malevolent like
wet clay in a
cemetery.

3.

The child plays with his
lunch box lid, the child
plays with his lunch
box lid, then with it
under his arm
he runs, he runs.

4.

The dog's ears prick up
whenever he hears their
voices.

The Inspiration of Trees

'A fool sees not the same tree that a wise man sees.'
– William Blake

My neighbour hated this imported
drought-resistant, fire-retardant tree
but knew its common names of
Flame of the Forest, Fireball Tree
and Fountain Tree.

This mattered little; he just wanted it gone,
excised from his half-acre backyard.

Watching from the kitchen window
while drinking the smell of coffee,
that wetty, dirty, muddy
tingling tar taste in my mouth,
he climbed that tree
with rain-wet-touched feet
not gripping like an old woman's
fragile lemon-coloured teeth.

He cut, adzed the African tulip tree
(*Spathodea Campanulata*) to a metre
above its dirt base, then tarred it like
some nerveless gangrenous stump so it
resembled an iodised streaked limb then
stood and lit one cigarette after another,
tip to tip like a caterpillar redtiptoredtip,
each near dead cigarette starting the next
and that African tulip, its blatant blossoms
of frightful orange spoke of throbbing

coloured life, each thick brown-sheathed
peduncle dripping with dew, I'd seen these
peduncles bound just below those drip-blooming
buds of orange, seen these peduncles bundled
together like the fasces of the Roman magistrates,
tied with coloured florists' ribbon and waiting in
big blue buckets, hand-painted milk curd canisters,
waiting, these spathe-shaped calyx of flowers,
a bunch of them, waiting, for some young man to
trollop part past, stop, and buy to excite his sweetheart.

Often I'd sit on the back pavers Dad and I laid,
watch Nature's day drool its steady supply of time,
time that I was loosing, time that Dad had already lost,
then sudden as crevice funnelled wind on some
brittle cold Alpine slope or a dark push of breeze
down a blackened blind narrowed alley, sudden as
things that come so far unexpected, only their sound
jinked into memory's side wall – the bird just arrived,
came and stopped, the swoosh of body through air,
its black and white and yellow-stained wings
already pulled back knife blade straight, retracted
in Folsom point head expectation, the brain full
of spigot-shaped desire, is it smell or colour or both
that has this bird riding the sky's waist then snap
sudden like a trapdoor spiders instant fear and fault
of nerve the bird is beak first in the burnt orange
tulip cavity, suck breathing juice pollen with its

brush-tipped tongue, doing it like first sex in its
slow-motion effects on lasting memory, while time's
lonely eyes move in slow perpetuity, it was much
like this as a young boy lying on my bed and
gazing up into the rest of my life, I'd see the
two planes fishing line hung from a double
screwdriver dug hole in the ceiling, watch two
grey model planes, a B52 bomber and a
Flying Fortress, my favourite, watch them
bob-slow about, about bob-slow, bob about
slow, slow-bob about as if they were happy,
their nose cones embedded in someone
else's reasons and soon I'd play a different
tune with my eyelids half closed and time's
idle wanton hand in its ridiculous need to do
things slow, time's idle wanton hand
humouring my needs as I undid my belt –
then those sudden tremulous sortie
seconds of pleasure, but what actually
is pleasure, perhaps this bird knows
more of happiness and pleasure.

Perhaps pleasure and happiness is
the floating above sun-buttered fields
with thoughts of long flight or that
sudden drawing back of wings as it
slow hit, care-plunged the soft wet
tissue of orange tulip fold, folds of
velvet wet flesh sun tuned and wind
touch tickled under sky's wide-eyed gaze.

Or is it the gentle piano thoughts,
the ivory tinklings of inspiration
of the whistling trees or birds gibbering
about the colours of Nature, colours
so tight in their tincturing of shades
that they distract all manner of things,
slow everything down to a muffle of time.

Is not Nature many tiny parts, minute
engines running, moving so slightly like
a drum skin quibbling in excitement
or a bellows just breathing ready.

The day was changing as the moon
halted on the sky like a congealed
milked tear and the curse of the wind
unwound itself in tatters in tree branches,
the stars hidden, buried deep like cold
old bone fragments as clouds sashayed
about stroking the sky with moist fingers
as other birds in hurried late afternoon
peak hour tree to tree traffic
watched and gossiped, wincing at the
sound of tension of tightening rope on trunk,
the noise like a cork being eased and prised,
eased and prised from a wine bottle's neck or
the sharp squeal of old dried sand underfoot.

As afternoon shadows shivered beside the
kneeling trees the glass coffins of my thoughts
and the tight crossbow of my sight recorded
the cold cutting memory of this event, an event
that will enter memory's crowded street and
later as darkness trains in become the
black gravity of more troubling thoughts.
This tree had survived the wind whipping
and sun scorching of the long drought's
open decree.

And now 3.14 p.m., the sun
loosing its rich red glisten,
I stood and watched, it was 3.14 p.m. plus
a few dribbled extra seconds when the
tree ceased to be a tree.

I was left with the reminder of the
expression, a dual scar on my retinas,
a hideous narrow eyed look of
false pleasure and fake happiness on
his face as he stood and stared into
the sky at the space where the tree had
been, stood there staring and smoking,
staring and smoking, staring into the
sky at the place where the tree had been
and there was not a bird in sight and
everything seemed so silent.

And the memory of my father as a seven-year-
old asleep in the old house at Buranda,
when a leaf drifted through the veranda
louvres settling on his mattress, waking
him in the middle of night with a thieving
tickle and a creeping touch at the underside
of his knee.

He placed that browning half palm-sized
gum leaf under an old black rock at the
bottom of the backstairs, the year, 1933.

I went outside and found one of those
peduncles, carried it inside to
place, to shut, to trap in the middle of
my most favourite book –
The Kon Tiki Expedition
by Thor Heyerdahl.

Between pages 114 & 115 I placed the now
fainting peduncle, squeezing the book shut.
Perhaps ten, fifteen, maybe twenty years
on my daughter, my son or someone else
will gather this book and notice the buckle
and bend of pages, the wave like turn of
compressed paper as if the book had been
shelved in water.

And inside, the flattened compressed
flower, its water-coloured purpled-pink
and oranged-brown juices
stained into the printed pages, bled
into the pages' texture and with this
a record, a story.

The bird is a New Holland honeyeater (*Phylidonyris Novaehollandiae*).

Warmth

It was the heat of our bodies,
you lying face down atop my
back, piggybacking sexuality,
it was the heat, like curtains
saturated with summer, heavy
with warmth, and as if pulling
them aside the sun played the
show of beauty of your body,
the love lines, the delicate
purple-blue veins at the upper
reaches of your thighs, the
exquisite tracks where my
tongue stroked slowly back
and forth to those sweat
tasting pockets of flesh,
tiny caverns of pleasure,
that now draws my eyes
thoughts. It was your shape,
smaller, lighter, you were like
a pencil outline drawn on my
flesh, so soft on my back
and your heartbeat a slow
soft hammering into my flesh,
matching the pulse of my
breath and then when you
kissed my neck, butterfly kisses
open and wet, I rolled
you over and off, the fullness
of your body like winter sun
ripened fruit and as you craned

your head back into the pillow,
the sculpture of your neck was
exposed to my tongue, you
pushed yourself up at me,
the gentle firmness of your
belly touching mine.

Days and Counting

'This life which you live and have lived, must be lived by you once again and innumerable times more; and there will be nothing new in it, but every pain and every joy and every thought and every sigh must come again to you. The eternal hourglass will again and again be turned and you with it, you grain of dust.' – Friedrich Nietzsche

It was the black gravity of my thoughts
that had me walking the complex of
45 units and counting each
paling on the entire fence.

The rusting nails in each paling like bleeding
ciphers or dark hidden eyes of discontent.

Two men arrived with blue yellow coloured
drills like huge whirring bumblebees, they began
screwing galvanised screws beside swollen rusted
nail heads, not replacing those sickly nails, but
leaving them to remain as staining seeps of rust,

14,981 palings, 54,930 nails and only 9,962 screws.
Watching the men I was more inclined to see
things in detail through the black gravity of
my thoughts.

On average a man will live for about 26,645
days before he dies – and to think those nails are
still alive, and what of the hard half palm-sized
gum leaf that my Dad as a kid placed under the
big black rock beside his backstairs back in 1933
on that night the leaf had drifted in through the

veranda window settling on his mattress waking
him in the middle of the night with a thieving tickle
and a creeping touch on the underside of his leg.

Dad lived for 29,736 days, but that leaf is still
there under the black rock, the nails are still there
and I am still here counting.

After That First Time

'All that remains of her
Now is pure womanly.'
– Thomas Hood, *The Bridge of Sighs*

She tries to disown the spotted fading stains of blood
but after a couple days of re-noticing and staring she
cuts that small portion, cuts and rips that small section
from the body of the off-white sheet, she cuts and rips
quickly with scissors in a gentle but jagged kind of way
and then begins folding it without touching the reminder,

that spread out blob of human ink, she folds it gingerly
with her own sad respect until it is bumpy flat, then sits
it on her upturned slightly bent palm, looks at it and then
places it down on the dining table then walks to the old
bookcase, sliding slowly a dusty book from the shelf –

Dubliners, James Joyce, 1914, first edition, signed to
Dorothea Mackellar, Rome, in faded fountain blue ink.

(And she thinks, how valuable this book that begs the
question, did they have a relationship in Rome, and
remember, she did go on to write a novel titled *Rome*.)

Gently she opens the book at page 173, halfway through
the story titled Grace, and pushes the folded off-white
fabric into the book right up to the stitched spine then
closes it briskly, placing the book back into the gap on

the shelf as she wipes tears on the collar of her cardigan
and feels its zipper cold and jagged on her cheek and at
the same time remembers hearing in the dark him unzipping...

Boot Scraper Mess

'What we call evil is simply ignorance bumping its head in the dark.' – Henry Ford

His mother said religion was important to a clean structured life, doctored he said, the dribble of glibness already at his chin, before even the words took challenge with the wall-to-wall carpet reality

of everyday thoughts. Throughout life he had catalogued heavy cast-iron feelings of guilt through the sweaty fingertips of daily thoughts. He was sick of the infantile doings of people, neighbours,

family, siblings, all that endeavouring to do things cautionary, to be moral, mental fitness in their simple hideous bodies of tissue, bone and fluids, without throwing caution to wind's rusted blade or

tarnishing one's soul a little in the sins of wet flesh or even living life to its tumescent fullest. Often he recalled his father's words: 'Wipe all those bad thoughts away before entering our home,

wipe them away' as he scraped his boot soles on the wrought iron boot scraper forged in the shape of cross, positioned at the base of the front steps, left boot to the left crossbar, right

boot to the right crossbar. The older he became the more he'd wonder who would make a boot scraper in the distinct shape of a cross, perhaps some wantonly donkeyed religious steeped fanatic who'd

too frequently assassinated his faith and glory above the drapery shop after the 20-second walk from the Hotel Abbs opposite late on a Friday night, 'The two twin deeds of evil in our main street' his mother had often piously sermonised. And his father late at night with the little hickory-handled spade shovelling the day's boot mess into the farthermost corner of the back garden, a neat pile roughly

pyramided into the junction point of the fence. He remembers him wandering the backyard, his voice drawn up through the veranda window on the night's bay breeze, his father saying over and over

'Wherever you go there's evil, wherever you go there's evil.' And that forever indelible sound of him wiping his hands on his oilskin trousers, so similar to the priest turning the pages of the big red book.

My Brother Visits Home

to Robert Adamson and Anthony Lawrence

'Youth would be an ideal state if it came a little later in life.'– Earl Asquith

Prologue

'When I first arrived a little grey-brown speckled sparrow would strike his beak at the machine hole drilled wire infused glass, even sticking his beak in the holes, I'd watch him, but now (if it's still him) he just shits on the window cavity ledge and flies off.' Prisoner 471 A.

1. Our Old Mother (Mary Altise)

Recently he watched her walk up
the street, the gate closed gingerly
in arthritic endeavour, the old
numbers in white and black paint
still having that new wet acrylic look.

But it's those lake cold eyes that hunger
his thoughts and constantly sauté them
in bewonderment, what is it
that makes him shiffle her past,
jigsawing fictive moment to fictive
moment to a running remembered picture
right up to her now octogenarian life.

Her own eyes seem to be questing a warm
meaning for the need of this stuttering,
shuffling inch *maidan* walk up the street.

He watches the trek, her back becoming
thinner in the dry cold distance, she
looks somehow pallid and weightless,
he imagines the air through which
she travels has a calm neutral
quenching stillness about it and
she never looks back.

Sometimes her figure resembles the shape
of a candle flame, upright and unmoving
just the burning urge from within, dousing
his dizzying thoughts in its sheer singular
monotony of uncompromising peace and
tranquillity but then there is movement in
her distant shape, not fluid movement but
half-tight like an over-wound clock or a
rusted hinge that moves some few creaking
fractions with its periodic tinny squeal.
Other days with hushed rain falling and
a lowering mist she still does the walk
and out of some peculiar need he watches and
listens to rain snuffling in the downpipes,
the sky cindered, fragile and lonely, and too
often there's the soft detonation of his heartbeat,
ta-stump, ta-stump, ta-stump, ta-stump.

She arrives back with a pig-coloured
complexion from exertion and there's
no sign of the tense trembling hands in
tune with the twittering bottom lip.

With this general tipsiness gone
her thoughts are more awake
but will soon slowly flicker and fade,
to a drawl of blurred thought.

2. Our Old Father (Patrick Peter)

He does little each day but natter to the
rose bushes and wander the front yard
nurturing things with his slowness.

A huddle of cloud mass in the left
east corner of the sky contrasts with
the soft heaping of wrinkles on his forehead.

Old straining eyes, squinted, constricted,
registering twin disdain from the seeped
in corners of each socket, eyes rinsed,

emptied of life, ninety years of black
and white Polaroid memories hidden
deep in the still tattoo-blue irises.

It wasn't enjoyment watching him move,
just like her frayed movement,
there was little refinement in the
shapes and shudders his body made as he
tended the green quivering flesh of his
beloved plants with his buckled aged hands,
flicking and squeezing the fat little aphids,
their body's yellow insides nicotining
his thumb and index finger, then the
thick yellow draught of a cough
coughed into his little dying mushroom-
shaped fist, a brief glimpse of his
straw-coloured teeth and the slight shake
as he is lost inside his ill-fitting frame
of downcast clothes that match the
ashen dishwater colour of his hair.

That cough from deep within the saggedly
loose lungs like a sad breeze blowing out of
a soddenly heavy hessian looking windsock,
and that terrible wet sound of sucking air.

After each cough there is a pause as if air
is drawn over a fold, lumped crease in his
lungs and this image somehow matches his
bent, lazily shaped question mark like body.

Inside the house his footfall as he moves
has a dead echo, out here he robot
shuffles about, and sometimes with the
same sudden intensity as a sharp needle
there's the septic odour of his breath,
and occasionally he looks, those stand
motionless eyes with eyelids thin as an
insect's wing, but it is always those old
tattoo-blue blobs of irises and the
splintered grin that stops ones thoughts
in their rusty tracks, conjuring hopes
for life and the future.

3. The Older Brother (Me, the Author)

I tell it as I see it, my brother and
his forlorn cold moods, his patient
determination in all its difficulty to
visit my parents as often as he can,
seeing them ageing in slow motions
half-peace and me unable to properly
talk or meet all three until 2012, the
end of my cringing incarceration, but
only able, only able to slowly read
and reread the telling letters that
all three of my people keep sending.

What am I left with but the telltale
frayed ends of memories in their snagged
splintered loneliness, I often stand like a
hatstand without hats trying to germinate
an attempt to contact them, to put pen's blood
of ink on shivering paper sheets, but all I do is
hesitate like a wary mud wasp forever hovering.

And today off in the distance some old codger
is burning rubbish in his backyard contrary
to the council regulations and as the Irish
writer John Banville wrote in his book *Eclipse*
'and the licorice smell of smoke and cinders'
and that's about all that is memorable about today.

'Once we are destined to live out our lives in the prison of
our mind, our one duty is to furnish it well.' – Peter Ustinov

Epilogue

'I no longer scratch the weeks on the wall with a spoon's lip's
edge but count remember and remember count the memories
of my brother, my mother and my father as the weeks creep
into time's ever ending.' Prisoner 471A.

People I See Walking

In photographs he'd have those neon tail-light eyes; in everyday life he's always swallowing.

With the grey glint of impending rain in the colour of her clothes, she hangs onto a cold smile.

An old man, with a fuddle of a walk and electric hands that always move, gives a wafer of a grin as damp clouds still the afternoon darkness.

A teenager too old for her youth knows the fog and shadow of other people's sins; she walks with her second face gripped in her left palm.

The child of three, happy with the mirth of his fumbling learning steps, giggles up at his mother-her eyes are cherry-sparked embers of delight.

An old woman full of perfume and fabric, arms weighted with bangles, bits of glitter and chink; her husband a Vietnam Veteran by his T-shirt.

The would-be ballerina with the tight triple hand-span waist and hair the colour of wet sand walks with a limp.

The spruiker outside the electrical store has tired doorway eyes and sloping shoulders.

With winter coming the merchant banker has hope stuck deep in his jacket pockets.

Like a matinee idol the young man ogles everything with mayhem eyes; he's looking for tricks.

With silver briefcase he has an uncanny logo of a smile as he reads *The Financial Review*.

A schoolboy, the stillness of his eyes like settled water, that stillness lost in the critique of his life medication, dotted to the limits in his blood stream.

And right now I've stopped outside the Irish Club…

Knocks At the Door and Poetry

for Julian

He came to the door offering something
that would afford him the warm pay cheque

at the end of a relentless week, for me it was
the mundane of seeing a short man in clothes of

no real ardour standing tapping gently, not
confidently but as a sick woodpecker might,

tapping, hoping that each tap would incise
and excite my needs, I'd sign up without

hesitation, but all I could do was tell him,
No, I was writing a poem, and like some

over the horizon flying machine a look
of delight came to his face, he was happy,

surprised that I'd given him a reason,
that I was indeed doing something as

important as what he was doing. He
asked me my name and I his.

Acknowledgements

Poems in this collection have previously appeared in the following publications: *Etchings, Idiom 23, LiNQ, The New England Review, Poetry Portraits, Southerly, Studio, Stylus Poetry Journal, The Big Weekend, The Canberra Times, The Stalking Tongue, The West Australian, Wet Ink*, ABC Radio National and in the anthology *The Henry Kendall Poetry Award 2006*.

'After that first Time' won the 2006 Apollo Poetry Award; 'The Dirigible over Suburbia Circa 1985' won the 2004 Dubbo National Poetry Prize and was commended in the 2003 W.B. Yeats Poetry Prize; 'Hammered into Heaven' won second prize in the 2003 W.B. Yeats Poetry Prize and was highly commended in the 2004 FAW John Shaw Neilson Poetry Award; 'Boot Scraper Mess' won third prize in the 2006 R.T. Edwards Poetry Award; 'Days and Counting' was highly commended in the 2007 C.J. Dennis Literary Awards; Drifting' was highly commended in the 2007 C.J. Dennis Literary Awards and short-listed in the 2004 Newcastle Poetry Prize; 'Walking Crop Circle' was highly commended in the 2005 New England Review Poetry Competition and also highly commended in the 2005 Bauhinia Literary Awards; 'White Hat' was highly commended in the 2004 R.T. Edwards Poetry Award; 'Moon Spit' was highly commended in the 2004 C.J. Dennis Literary Award; 'The Crooked Floor' was highly commended in the 2001 Tom Collins Poetry Prize; 'The Inspiration of Trees' was Commended in the 2006 Rolf Boldrewood Poetry Award; 'In Downpours' was commended in the 2003 W.B. Yeats Poetry Prize; 'Reading Your Book' was commended in the 2006 MPU International Poetry Competition and commended in the 2006

Shoalhaven Literary Award and shortlisted in the 2005 FAW John Shaw Neilson Poetry Award; 'The Continual Breaking of Fragile Glass' was highly commended in the FAW National Literary Awards and shortlisted in the 2004 Newcastle Poetry Prize; 'That Night at the Powerhouse' was shortlisted in the 2003 Julie Lewis Literary Awards.

The author gratefully acknowledges writer-in-residencies at St Saviour's College (2004), Brisbane Boys' College (2003), Coomera Anglican College (2003), Nudgee State School (2002), Marist College Ashgrove (2002) and Hillbrook Anglican School (2001), where many of these poems were written.

Special thanks must go to Emeritus Professor Maurice Brearley for his encouragement and advice.

www.ingramcontent.com/pod-product-compliance
Lightning Source LLC
Chambersburg PA
CBHW070321120526
44590CB00017B/2767